teach me about

Mommies and Daddies

Copyright © Joy Berry, 2020
Reprinted by permission. Originally Published 1986

The statements and opinions expressed in this work are solely those of the author and do not reflect the thoughts or opinions of the publisher.

Every effort has been made to trace the copyright holder(s) and obtain permission to reproduce all elements of this material.

All rights reserved. No part of this book may be reproduced or used in any manner without the prior written permission of the copyright owner, except for the use of brief quotations in a book review. For inquiries or to request permission, contact the publisher at rights@lemurpress.com

ISBN 978-1-63617-126-5

Published by Lemur Press
lemurpress.com

LEMUR PRESS

teach me about

Mommies and Daddies

By JOY BERRY

Illustrated by Bartholomew

LEMUR PRESS

Like you, your mommy and daddy have bodies.

Like you, they do things to keep their bodies well.

They

- breathe
- eat and drink
- go to the bathroom
- exercise
- rest

Like you, your mommy and daddy have bodies that do things that may seem strange. Their bodies

- snore
- sneeze and cough
- hiccup and burp
- throw up

Like you, your mommy and daddy have feelings. Sometimes they feel happy. Sometimes they feel

- sad
- angry
- upset

Like you, your mommy

and daddy need love.

They need to love other people.

They need other people

to love them.

Like you, your mommy
and daddy need to work.
They also need to play.

Like you, your mommy and daddy do not know everything there is to know. They learn new things all the time.

Like you, your mommy

and daddy are not perfect.

They have accidents.

They also make mistakes.

In some ways your mommy
and daddy are **not** like you.
Your mommy and daddy
are bigger than you.
Because they are bigger,
they are stronger than you.

Your mommy and daddy

are older than you.

They have lived

much longer than you.

Because they have lived longer,

they have learned more than you.

They know more than you know.

Your mommy and daddy are able to take care of you because they are

- bigger,
- stronger,
- older, and
- wiser

than you are.

Your mommy and daddy do many things to take care of you. There are many things you need in order to

- be healthy, and
- grow.

Your mommy and daddy take care of you by making sure that you get the things you need.

Your mommy and daddy take care of you by keeping you safe. They do their best to make sure that nothing harmful happens to you.

Your mommy and daddy take care of you by telling you what you need to do. They tell you what you need to do because they do not want you to

- hurt yourself,
- hurt other people, or
- damage anyone's belongings.

Your mommy and daddy take care of you by telling you what you are **not** to do.

They tell you no because they do not want you to

- hurt yourself,
- hurt other people, or
- damage anyone's belongings.

Your mommy and daddy take care of you because you are their child and they love you very much.

helpful hints for parents about

Mommies and Daddies

Dear Parents:

The purpose of this book is
- to encourage children to be more empathetic and understanding toward their parents by reviewing the human similarities that children share with their parents, and
- to explain that parents are qualified for the parental role and are entitled to a certain amount of control over their children because of the differences between parents and children.

You can best implement the purpose of this book by
- reading it to your child, and
- reading the following *Helpful Hints* and using them whenever applicable.

CONFIDENCE

Choices

Parents need to know that there is no *one* perfect way to raise children. Each person needs to parent in a way that is consistent with his or her own personality. You can be the best possible parent to your child by using these guidelines:

1. Evaluate the child-rearing philosophy you inherited from your parents.
2. Commit yourself to perpetuating the positive aspects of your parents' philosophy.
3. Be aware of parenting behavior that you do not wish to repeat.
4. Consider yourself at risk for abusive behavior as a parent if you were abused as a child, are under unusual stress, or misuse alcohol or drugs.
5. Break the cycle of abuse by
   - learning all you can about good parents from other adults, reading, and attending classes;
   - avoiding alcohol and drugs; and
   - seeking professional help if you feel you cannot control your behavior with your child.

Educate yourself

A great deal of information is available from books and classes on early childhood. Parents can educate themselves by learning about
- child development
- nutritional needs of young children
- how to promote their child's learning
- health and behavior problems

UNIQUENESS
Your child is a separate person, a unique individual.

Blame
Parents need not blame themselves for their child's problems. While mother and father are two very important factors in a child's life, many factors contribute to an individual's problems.

Credit
Parents cannot take credit for all of their child's successes. Each individual has a right to full credit for his or her own success. Parents can certainly contribute to and take pride in a child's success, but achievement belongs to the individual.

ENJOYMENT
Why are grandparents able to enjoy their grandchildren so much? One reason is that they have learned an important lesson about children: to enjoy them when they're young because they really do grow up. Parents can lose sight of that fact in meeting the urgent, day-to-day demands of raising children.

Secondhand success
Mothers and fathers who look to their children to make them feel successful rob themselves and their children of opportunities for individual success. When children are made the focus of all their parents' energy and motivation, there may be little left over for the parents' personal fulfillment. Children can benefit from the experience of their own struggle for achievement and have a right to claim its reward for themselves.

One to one
Many parents feel a need to prove their worth as "good parents" by arranging activities for their children. "Devoted" parents shuttle their busy

kids from lessons to clubs to recreation with friends. Children need activities, but good relationships between parents and children are built on quality time *together*. Quality time means one-to-one interaction, such as
- conversation,
- sharing an activity, or
- spending time together.

Take the time to know the person who is your child and to share yourself. Get to know each other as people apart from your roles.

SELF-SACRIFICE

Putting your child first, sacrificing your own needs to meet your child's needs, is both instinctive and learned behavior of good parenting. However, mothers and fathers *must* use their own judgment to balance meeting their own needs with those of their children.

Unrealistic expectations

Without realizing it, parents can have expectations of a payoff for their sacrifices. Sometimes these expectations are greater than a child can be expected to fulfill.

One-way giving

Many times the child is unaware of parental expectations and fails to reciprocate for the parents' sacrifices. Parents continue giving and the child continues receiving.

Resentment

Parents who sacrifice a great deal for a child who fails to meet their expectations of return may feel unappreciated and unconsciously resentful. This resentment undermines a good parent-child relationship. To avoid resenting your child, be aware of your
- unrealistic expectations to be a self-sacrificing parent;

- willingness to balance meeting your own needs with meeting your child's needs;
- unrealistic expectations for a payoff from your child, either now or later;
- feelings of resentment before they build and threaten your relationship with your child.

PARENTAL RULES

Some problems associated with the roles of mother and father can be summarized by the following common myths:

Myth #1. Parents alone know what is best for their children at all times. As a separate individual, a child has thoughts, feelings, desires, and aspirations that are all his or her own. You can offer your child an opportunity to express that individuality by giving him or her choices from an early age. Let the child choose between two possibilities when choice is appropriate. Choices that could negatively affect his or her health or well-being are not appropriate for a young child to make. A child learns to make appropriate choices to satisfy individual needs through practice. Use your child's input when making decisions that will affect his or her life.

Myth #2. Parents must appear perfect in order for their children to respect them and feel secure. Parents who try to present a model of perfection are setting up themselves and their children for failure. Perfection is too high an expectation for parents to place on themselves and by their example on their children. Children need a model for how to handle failure in a positive, productive way. By making mistakes and admitting them, parents give their children permission to make mistakes and still feel love and approval. This kind of parental acceptance can provide a child with a foundation for lifelong security.

Myth #3. Parents must be in control of their children at all times. Children begin learning to control their bodies and their environment from birth. Parents can observe slow but steady progress in their children's control and an obvious desire to achieve more. This desire for mastery of their environment sometimes causes children to take on more than they can handle, requiring parents to step in and take back some control. A gradual shift in control from parent to child is a necessary process which makes it possible for the young adult to competently assume control of his or her life at an appropriate time. Control is proportionate to responsibility. The more responsibility a child assumes, the more control the child can and should assume.

Myth #4. Parents have the sole responsibility of meeting their children's needs. Parents have a responsibility to be aware of their children's needs and to see that, as far as possible, the child's needs are met. This does not mean, however, that a parent has sole responsibility for meeting all of a child's needs. Assuming that kind of responsibility would leave parents with little time or energy for meeting personal needs. Parents need to use their resources to provide for their children's needs at no loss to themselves or to the child. Parental resources may include any of the following:
- payment of money in return for services to your child, such as baby-sitting, music, dance, or swim lessons;
- exchange of your services for services to your child, such as baby-sitting, tutoring, carpooling, or lessons;
- donations of services from friends or relatives willing to share the parental responsibility for your child.

CONFLICT

Many parents believe that a model family is free of conflicts. In the "perfect family," model parents and children never experience negative feelings toward one another and therefore never express negative emotions. There is no arguing or fighting in the peaceful, model family. This model, of course, cannot exist in the real world.

Permission
Parents must give themselves and their children permission to experience family conflict. This permission does not invite conflict, but merely acknowledges that conflict exists in any family. Conflict offers an opportunity to
- air grievances,
- make changes, and
- increase family solidarity.

Children learn to resolve differences and negotiate agreements by working through family conflicts.

Solutions
For many children television provides the only model for family interaction outside their own family. But television presents an unrealistic model of family conflicts that are resolved in the 30- to 60-minute format of the program. Viewing and discussing TV programs with your child can determine what lessons are learned from television. Real solutions to family conflicts require permission to experience the conflict and a commitment to negotiate solutions that are acceptable to all the family members involved.

CPSIA information can be obtained
at www.ICGtesting.com
Printed in the USA
BVHW050441021220
594503BV00001B/14